HALLOWEEN

by Joyce K. Kessel

illustrations by Nancy Carlson

On My Own
HOLIDAYS

€ Carolrhoda Books, Inc./Minneapolis

This book is available in two editions:
Library binding by Carolrhoda Books, Inc., a division of Lerner Publishing Group
Soft cover by First Avenue Editions, an imprint of Lerner Publishing Group
241 First Avenue North
Minneapolis, MN 55401 U.S.A.

Website address: www.lernerbooks.com

Library of Congress Cataloging-in-Publication Data

Kessel, Joyce K.
    Halloween / by Joyce K. Kessel ; illustrated by Nancy Carlson. (Rev. ed.)
      p.   cm. — (On my own holidays)
    Summary: Introduces the history of Halloween, the meaning of its symbols, and the ways in which we celebrate it today.
    ISBN: 0-87614-933-6 (lib. bdg. : alk. paper)
    ISBN: 1-57505-582-1 (pbk. bdg. : alk. paper)
    1. Halloween—Juvenile literature. [1. Halloween. 2. Holidays.] I. Carlson, Nancy L., ill. II. Title. III. Series.
    GT4965 .K47 2004
    394.2646—dc21   2002007512

Manufactured in the United States of America
1 2 3 4 5 6 - JR - 09 08 07 06 05 04

to Dad and Dee — J.K.K.

to my mother and father — N.C.

Fall has always been
a special time of year.
It is a time to give thanks.
The crops are in.
There is enough food for all.

But hundreds of years ago,

fall was also a time to feel afraid.

People felt the sun grow weaker.

They watched the days grow shorter.

They saw plants dying.

Long ago, that frightened people.
They thought evil powers
were pushing the sun away.

The Celts were people

who lived over 2,000 years ago.

Most of them lived

in Great Britain and Ireland.

The Celts had many gods.

One was named Samhain.

He was the god of death.

His special night was October 31.

That was the Celts' New Year's Eve.

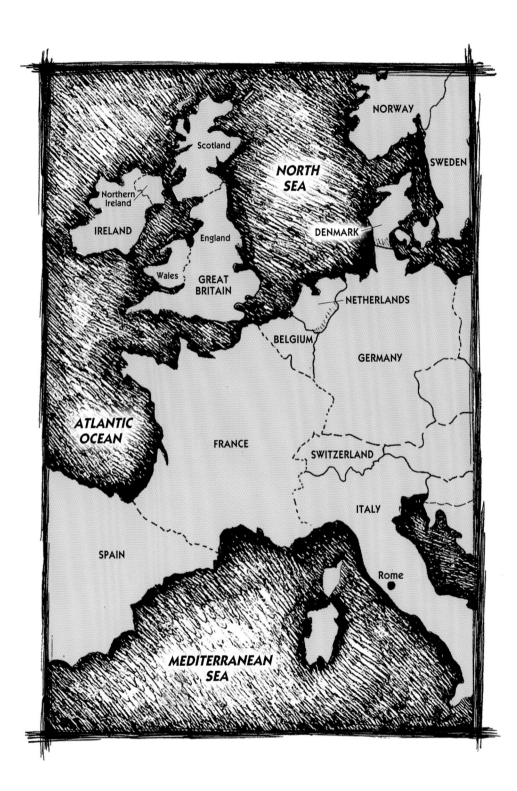

The Celts believed

Samhain came to earth that night.

He let the dead come back, too.

The Celts made large fires.

They burned animals as gifts for Samhain.

Some of them wore costumes
made from animals' heads and furs.
Samhain's night was a frightening time.
It marked the beginning of winter.
It became the beginning of our Halloween.

In the year A.D. 43,

the Romans conquered the Celts.

The Romans also had many gods.

One was named Pomona.

She was the goddess of fruit.

Her festival was in the fall.

It came right after Samhain's night.

But Pomona's festival was a happy time.

It was a time to give thanks

to all the gods.

Apples were important to Pomona.

So Romans gave apples

to their gods of rain and fire.

They wanted to thank them

for not harming the crops.

13

The Romans ruled the Celts
for about 400 years.
During that time,
Pomona's and Samhain's festivals
got mixed up.
They became one festival.

In the 1800s, many people
moved to the United States.
Some came from
Great Britain and Ireland.
That was where the Celts had lived.
They brought their holidays with them.
One of those holidays was Halloween.

17

Black Cats

Think of all the black cats
you see on Halloween.
Black cats standing beside
jack-o'-lanterns.
Black cats on witches' brooms.
Some people think
black cats bring bad luck.

The Celts believed black cats
had once been people.
They thought bad magic
had changed them into cats.
The Celts captured black cats
with silver ropes.
They wanted to keep them
to protect church treasures.

Jack-o'-Lanterns

We got the jack-o'-lantern from Ireland.

The Irish tell a story

about a man named Jack.

Jack was very bad.

He could not go to heaven.

So he was sent to hell.

But he played too many tricks there.

The devil got angry.

Finally, the devil sent Jack

out of hell, too.

Jack had no place to go.

He had to walk the earth forever.

All he owned was a little lantern.

The Irish called him
Jack of the Lantern.
So when we light up
pumpkins like lanterns,
we call them jack-o'-lanterns.

Trick-or-Treating

Trick-or-treating

came from Ireland, too.

Long ago, people believed in ghosts.

Clever Irish farmers made use of that.

They went to rich homes.

They asked for food.

If the rich people would not give any,

the farmers played tricks on them.

They might steal a gate.

They might move a wagon far away.

People thought ghosts

had played the tricks.

24

"We should be nicer," they said.

"Then the ghosts will leave us alone."

So they gave food to the farmers.

And the ghosts stayed away!

Ghosts

A ghost is a spirit of a dead person
that visits a living person.
Most people do not
believe in ghosts.
But long ago, most people did.
Ghosts have been part of Halloween
from its very beginning.

The Celts believed ghosts
visited earth on October 31.
People in other countries
also came to believe this.

There is a big cave in Ireland.

It is called the Hell-Gate of Ireland.

People once believed

this cave opened on Halloween.

Horrible ghosts flew out of it.

People thought the ghosts killed animals.

They believed the ghosts took babies, too.

Witches

A witch is a woman with magic powers.
Once the word *witch* could mean
a man or a woman.
Later, witches who were men
were called warlocks.

In Scotland, people once believed
all witches met on Halloween.
The devil called them together.
They danced all night.

Music was played
on the "devil's bagpipe."
This bagpipe was made
from hens' heads and cats' tails!

Apples

Apples became part of
Halloween when the Romans
conquered the Celts.
There are many apple games
to play on Halloween.

One Halloween game is called
snap apple.

People tie strings to apples.

They hang them from the ceiling.

Everyone takes turns.

They stand on a chair.

The apples swing back and forth.

The trick is to take a bite of one.

But you can't use your hands.

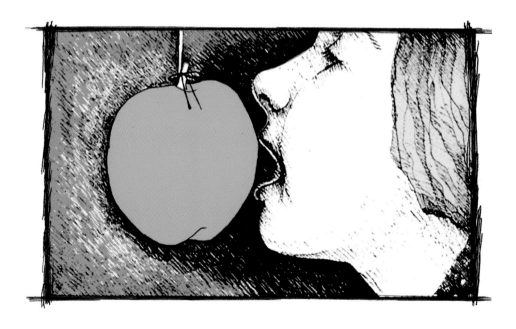

People often bob for apples
on Halloween.
Apples are put in a tub of water.
People try to catch one
in their teeth.
They hold their hands
behind their backs.
Another favorite Halloween game
is passing an apple
from one person to another.
You can't use your hands
in this game, either.
You must hold the apple
under your chin!

Fortune-Telling

Have you ever had your fortune told?

Maybe someone has read your palm.

Other people read tea leaves.

Fortune-tellers tell people

what might happen to them.

The Celts told fortunes
by looking through what was left
of burned animals.
These animals had been burned
as gifts for Samhain.

The Celts believed
the fortunes they told.
We tell fortunes
at Halloween, too.
But we don't really believe them.
We do it for fun.
The English called Halloween
Nutcracker Night.
Sweethearts threw nuts
into the fire.
Sometimes they exploded.
That meant a bad marriage.
Sometimes they burned quietly.
That meant a good marriage.

The Irish hide rings in food.

If you find the ring,

you will marry soon.

Bonfires

Have you ever been
to a Halloween bonfire?
The fire crackles.
It feels warm.
It smells good.
People sing songs.
They tell ghost stories.
It is a happy time.

But bonfires used to be very serious.

The Celts burned them for Samhain.

Later, people burned bonfires

all over Great Britain and Ireland

on Halloween.

They did this to frighten

ghosts and witches away.

In Scotland, people burned torches.

Then they ran through the streets.

They were trying to frighten witches.

43

Later, they made a big fire
with all the torches.

Then a man dressed up like a ghost.

He rode up on a horse.

The horse pulled a wagon.

In the wagon was a make-believe witch.

The people screamed.

They threw the witch into the fire!

While the witch burned, they danced.

People in Wales burned bonfires, too.
Each person would mark a stone.
They threw the stones into the fire.
Sometimes a stone was missing
the next morning.
People thought
the person who
marked the missing stone
would die that year.

The early reasons for Halloween
have disappeared.
Few people still believe
the dead come back.
But we carry on some of the old customs.

It's fun to pretend

we believe in witches and ghosts.

It's fun to tell scary stories

and go trick-or-treating.

It's fun to tell fortunes,

even if we don't really believe them.

In October, the dry leaves
whisper like witches.
Our bright jack-o'-lanterns
smile at our windows.
Halloween is a happy way
to say hello to winter.